It's My State!

MARYLAND

The Old Line State

Steven Otfinoski and Andy Steinitz

Cavendish
Square

New York

Published in 2015 by Cavendish Square Publishing, LLC
243 5th Avenue, Suite 136, New York, NY 10016

Library of Congress Cataloging-in-Publication Data
Otfinoski, Steven.
 Maryland / Steven Otfinoski, Andy Steinitz. — Third edition.
   pages cm. — (It's my state!)
 Includes index.
 ISBN 978-1-62712-743-1 (hardcover) ISBN 978-1-62712-745-5 (ebook)
 1. Maryland—Juvenile literature. I. Steinitz, Andy. II. Title.

F181.3.O84 2015
975.2—dc23

                    2014006981

Editorial Director: Dean Miller
Editor, Third Edition: Nicole Sothard
Art Director: Jeffrey Talbot
Series Designer, Third Edition: Jeffrey Talbot
Layout Design, Third Edition: Erica Clendening
Production Manager: Jennifer Ryder-Talbot

MARYLAND

CONTENTS

State Flower: Black-Eyed Susan

This small wildflower is also called the yellow daisy. It is hard to pick the flower without pulling the plant up by the roots because the stems are so tough.

State Crustacean: Blue Crab

The brackish, or slightly salty, water of the Chesapeake Bay is the perfect home for blue crabs. Steamed, sautéed, or cooked in crab cakes or soup, the blue crab is one of Maryland's favorite dishes.

State Bird: Baltimore Oriole

The male oriole's black and orange feathers are the colors of the coat of arms of the Calverts, the English family that founded Maryland. The Baltimore Orioles baseball team is named for this bird.

MARYLAND

State Tree: White Oak

The white oak was named the state tree of Maryland in 1941. The most famous white oak in Maryland was the Wye Oak. It grew in Talbot County for more than 450 years. The "Quiet Giant" measured nearly 32 feet (10 meters) around. It was downed by a storm in 2002.

State Dog: Chesapeake Bay Retriever

Maryland's state dog is very special. It is one of the few dog breeds native to the United States. It got its name because it is trained to retrieve game birds shot by hunters.

State Reptile: Diamondback Terrapin

This turtle lives in salty marshes along the Chesapeake Bay. It can be identified by the diamond-shaped rings on its shell. Each shell has a unique pattern. The terrapin is the mascot of the sports teams of the University of Maryland at College Park.

A view of the Chesapeake Bay from Tilghman Island.

The Old Line State

Maryland is the ninth-smallest state. For such a small state, it has a lot of people. Maryland's population was more than 5.7 million in 2010. That made it the 19th most populous state. Maryland has a lot of natural wonders to attract all those people—plains, hills, valleys, mountains, and ocean beaches. Forests cover two-fifths of the state. About 160 different kinds of trees thrive there. Maryland has one of the finest bays in the world—the Chesapeake Bay. Proud Marylanders say that their state has it all.

The Chesapeake Bay

No matter where you are in Maryland, you are never very far from water. The Chesapeake Bay nearly cuts the state in half. The region between the bay and the Atlantic Ocean is called the Eastern Shore. The bay is the largest estuary in North America. An estuary is an area where fresh river water and salty ocean water mix. Only 31 miles (50 kilometers) of the state face the Atlantic Ocean. The Chesapeake Bay, however, provides Maryland with a long and twisting shoreline that runs about 7,000 miles (11,200 km). The bay has many good harbors for boats.

Crab traps sit on a dock in Cape Charles, on the Chesapeake Bay.

Maryland Borders

North:	Pennsylvania
South:	District of Columbia
	Virginia
East:	Delaware
	Atlantic Ocean
West:	West Virginia
	Virginia

The name *Chesapeake* comes from the Algonquian word *Chesepiooc*. Some people say that was the name of a Native American village at the mouth of the bay. Others believe the word means "great shellfish bay." Either meaning fits the Chesapeake. For centuries, people have been catching oysters, crabs, and fish in its blue waters.

The Chesapeake provides a home and food for many different types of plants and animals. Fish of many types live in the bay and its marshes, wetlands, and tributaries.

More than four hundred rivers, flowing from six states, feed into the Chesapeake Bay. The largest are the Susquehanna River in the north and the Potomac River, which forms the state's southwestern border. Sixteen of Maryland's 23 counties border the Chesapeake. Annapolis, the state capital, is in Anne Arundel County on the bay's western shore.

There are no natural lakes in Maryland. All existing lakes have been made artificially by damming rivers. The largest of these, Deep Creek Lake, is 12 miles (19 km) long. It covers 3,900 acres (1,578 ha), and it has 65 miles (105 km) of shoreline. Deep Creek Lake is a popular place to swim and fish for bass, pike, and trout.

A daring kayaker paddles down one of the many rapids of the Great Falls on the Potomac River.

MARYLAND
COUNTY MAP

GARRETT

ALLEGANY

WASHINGTON

CARROLL

FREDERICK

HARFORD

CECIL

BALTIMORE

BALTIMORE CITY

KENT

HOWARD

MONTGOMERY

ANNE ARUNDEL

QUEEN ANNE'S

CAROLINE

TALBOT

PRINCE GEORGE'S

CHARLES

CALVERT

DORCHESTER

WICOMICO

SAINT MARY'S

SOMERSET

WORCESTER

Allegany County	75,087
Anne Arundel County	537,656
Baltimore County	805,029
Calvert County	88,737
Caroline County	33,066
Carroll County	167,134
Cecil County	101,108
Charles County	146,551
Dorchester County	32,618
Frederick County	233,385
Garrett County	30,097
Harford County	244,826
Howard County	287,085
Kent County	20,197
Montgomery County	971,777
Prince George's County	863,420
Queen Anne's County	47,798
St. Mary's County	105,151
Somerset County	26,470
Talbot County	37,782
Washington County	147,430
Wicomico County	98,733
Worcester County	51,454
Baltimore City	620,961

Maryland has 23 counties and one independent city (Baltimore). Source: U.S. Bureau of the Census, 2010

Anne Arundel County

Worcester County

An aerial view of Ocean City.

Marylanders enjoy all the water that surrounds them. Some like to sail boats in the bay, while others prefer to water-ski. Sport fishing is popular in the Atlantic Ocean, and many people enjoy catching crabs in the bay and rivers.

Plains, Plateaus, and Mountains

Maryland's varied landscape is divided into three land regions. The eastern part—which is split by the Chesapeake Bay—is called the Atlantic Coastal Plain. The area is dotted with marshes and swamps. Much of the fertile land is used for growing crops and raising chickens. The Atlantic Coastal Plain is home to Baltimore, Maryland's largest city. Ocean City, a popular beach town, is also located there. Only about 7,000 residents live in Ocean City year-round, but millions of tourists visit each summer.

Beyond the plains region stretches a wide area called the Piedmont. The plateau's hills and valleys contain most of the state's dairy farms.

The Appalachian Region is located in the western "panhandle." Two mountain ranges—the Alleghenies and Blue Ridge—are part of the larger Appalachian range. The region's apple orchards thrive in the cooler weather, and its forests provide many jobs. The Appalachians were formed about 230 million years ago. They are the oldest mountains in North America. At Hancock, Maryland, in the Appalachian Region, the state is less than 2 miles (3.2 km) wide from north to south. That is the narrowest width recorded in any state.

The Blue Ridge Mountains extend as far south as northern Georgia and cut across a narrow strip of Maryland. They form one of the loveliest areas of the state. Their name comes from the blue haze that appears to hang over the mountains. The Allegheny Mountains lie in the westernmost part of Maryland. At 3,360 feet (1,024 m), Backbone Mountain in the Alleghenies is the highest peak in the state.

The view from Annapolis Rock along the Appalachian Trail in the Blue Ridge Mountains.

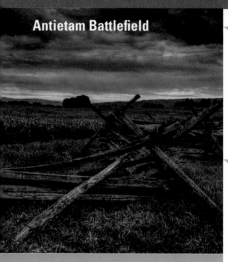

Antietam Battlefield

1. Antietam Battlefield

The Battle of Antietam was the bloodiest one-day battle of the Civil War. Today, the battlefield commemorates the event that took place on September 17, 1862. More than 300,000 people visit the site every year.

2. Deep Creek Lake

Deep Creek Lake is the largest inland lake in Maryland, and it is man-made! The lake, located in Western Maryland, is home to different types of birds and fish, and visitors enjoy the lake as well. It is a popular place to swim, boat, fish, and water-ski.

Fort McHenry National Monument

3. Fort McHenry National Monument

Fort McHenry is a star-shaped fort at which American soldiers successfully defended Baltimore Harbor from an attack by the British during the War of 1812. It is also the location at which Francis Scott Key wrote the words to the National Anthem.

4. Maryland Science Center

Named one of the best 10 science centers in America for families, the Maryland Science Center features exhibits that focus on dinosaurs, space, the blue crab, and much more. It is located at Baltimore's Inner Harbor.

Maryland Zoo

5. Maryland Zoo

The Maryland Zoo in Baltimore is the third oldest zoo in the United States. It is a 135-acre (55 ha) zoo that houses more than 1,500 animals. The exhibits at the Maryland Zoo are meant to replicate each animal's natural habitat.

6. NASA Goddard Space Flight Center

The Goddard Space Flight Center in Greenbelt offers programs, special events, and presentations that reflect the center's work in Earth science, astrophysics, heliophysics, planetary science, engineering, communication, and technology. Among the exhibits are interactive displays and models, satellites, and rocket flight hardware.

7. National Aquarium

The National Aquarium, in Baltimore's Inner Harbor, features more than 17,000 animals from 750 species of fish, birds, amphibians, reptiles, and mammals. Visitors can get up close and personal with sharks, jellyfish, and dolphins!

8. Ocean City

Marylanders love to go "downy owe-shun," which means to the beach at Ocean City. You can stroll the boardwalk, eat great seafood, go fishing for marlin, play the games at the arcades, enjoy miles of wide sand beaches, or take a trip to see the wild horses on Assateague Island.

9. Oriole Park at Camden Yards

Oriole Park at Camden Yards is home to Maryland's Major League Baseball (MLB) team, the Baltimore Orioles. Opened in 1992, the park is known for its old-fashioned design. It is a favorite among baseball enthusiasts.

10. USS *Constellation*

The USS *Constellation* is a sloop-of-war, or small warship, that patrolled waters during the Civil War and was used as a training vessel during WWI. Today, visitors can tour the ship and learn about its history and what life was like on board.

National Aquarium

Camden Yards

USS *Constellation*

A young hiker takes a break along the Appalachian Trail in Washington County. The 2,175-mile (3,500-km) trail stretches from Maine to Georgia.

The Old Line State

Some historians believe that George Washington himself gave Maryland its first nickname, the Old Line State. Washington was greatly impressed with the Maryland Line, the troops who fought bravely during the American Revolution [1775–1783].

Climate

Eastern Maryland can be hot and humid in summer. Average temperatures approach 90 degrees Fahrenheit (32 degrees Celsius) in July and August. The area has mild winters, thanks to warm ocean breezes created by the Gulf Stream. The Gulf Stream is a warm ocean current that flows north from the Gulf of Mexico. The mountainous region in Western Maryland is considerably cooler and gets the most snowfall in the state. Up to 110 inches (279 centimeters) of snow can fall in certain parts of the state every year. The state receives an average of 41 inches (104 cm) of rain a year.

Violent storms and hurricanes are rare in Maryland. An exception was Hurricane Agnes, which struck the Maryland coast in June 1972. In Maryland, the hurricane caused $110 million in damages and took 19 lives. In September 2003, Hurricane Isabel caused the worst flooding along the Chesapeake coast in seventy years. In Baltimore, water levels rose 8 feet (2.4 m). The storm caused $410 million in damages statewide.

Wildlife in Maryland

Maryland once had large wild animals such as cougars, elk, and bison. But people killed or drove away most of them. The only big mammal left in large numbers is the white-tailed deer. Black bears, once a rare site in Maryland, are becoming more common in the western mountains. They have even been spotted on the Eastern Shore. But if you walk through wooded areas, you are more likely to come upon many smaller animals, such as raccoons, muskrats, gray squirrels, and red foxes.

The Chesapeake Bay's marshes are home to thousands of water birds. They include many kinds of ducks, terns, and geese. The great blue heron can be found along the state's many rivers and streams, where it catches fish. With its long, pointed bill and thin, storklike legs, it is the largest American heron.

Maryland hunters stalk game birds, such as quail, mourning doves, ducks, and ring-necked pheasants. Hunters often use the state dog, the Chesapeake Bay retriever, to find the game birds they have shot. No one knows for sure how this dog breed developed in Maryland. One story goes that a British ship was wrecked off the coast in the early 1800s. Two Newfoundland dogs were saved from the ship and bred with local dogs. Over time, they produced a new breed.

Following Hurricane Isabel, a rescue boat motors down a flooded street in North Beach, on the western shore of the Chesapeake Bay.

A Chesapeake Bay retriever jumps a hurdle during an agility competition.

Bay retrievers are highly intelligent and very loyal dogs. Sometimes they are trained to sniff out drugs for law **enforcement** officers and to perform rescue work. These dogs are so friendly that they are brought to hospitals and nursing homes to cheer up patients.

Marylanders have not had as good a relationship with their state bird, the Baltimore oriole. The oriole was given protection under state law in 1882 and was further protected under the state's Nongame and **Endangered** Species Conservation Act in 1975. Despite these laws, the bird's population has been declining. Much of its habitat has been destroyed by the construction of offices, stores, and factories. Also, many orioles have died from eating insects containing poisonous pesticides.

The Chesapeake Bay is full of many kinds of fish—such as shad, drumfish, and the state fish, rockfish—that are fished commercially. In the ocean, sport fishers hook their lines to catch marlins, which resemble swordfish and can weigh up to 400 pounds (180 kilograms). In the rivers and streams, trout and perch are favorite catches. Marshes are home to the diamondback terrapin, Maryland's state reptile. Before laws were passed to protect them, diamondbacks were nearly hunted into extinction for their delicious meat.

The Wild Horses of Assateague Island

Perhaps Maryland's most interesting animals are the wild horses of Assateague Island. This long, narrow island sits off Maryland's Atlantic coast. Two million visitors come to Assateague Island National Seashore each year to see the horses.

How the horses got there is a mystery. One legend claims that a Spanish ship ran aground on the island many years ago, and the horses on board escaped. But many people now believe the horses are the **descendants** of workhorses that farmers brought to the island and let graze on the marsh grasses. The grasses are not very nutritious, so the horses of Assateague grow only to the size of ponies.

The wild horses still survive on the marsh grasses today. This has become a problem. The marsh grass holds the sand together to form dunes. If new dunes are not created, the ocean waters will eat away at the land. One day the island will be covered by water.

Scientists have developed ways to control the wild horse population. State workers shoot darts at the female horses, called mares. The darts contain a **vaccine** that prevents the mares from having babies. Each year, some of the horses are also rounded up and sold at auctions. These measures keep the number of horses down and help protect the island.

Wild horses take a drink at Assateague Island National Seashore.

Bald Cypress

Black-Eyed Susan

Bobcat

1. Bald Cypress

The bald cypress tree is a relative of the sequoia. The Battle Creek Cypress Swamp Nature Center in Southern Maryland has one of the northernmost stands of bald cypress in the United States. Some of the trees are more than 500 years old.

2. State Bird: Baltimore Oriole

Baltimore orioles live in Maryland and other parts of the eastern United States only during the summer. In winter, some of them live in the southeastern U.S., but most fly further south looking for warmer weather. Orioles are omnivores, and they eat both insects and fruit.

3. State Flower: Black-Eyed Susan

Black-eyed susans are yellow flowers with a brown-purple center. They grow in open woods, fields, along the road, and in gardens. They often grow to become over three feet (91 cm) tall, and they bloom mostly during late summer and early fall.

4. State Crustacean: Blue Crab

The blue crab is known for its bright blue claws and olive green shell. Living on the bottom of the Chesapeake Bay, blue crabs feed on oysters, clams, mussels, and fish. The Maryland blue crab became the State Crustacean in 1989.

5. Bobcat

Bobcats look like house cats, but they are twice the size and have dark spots. They can be found in Western Maryland. They eat birds, squirrels, mice, and other small animals. Bobcats are named for their short, bobbed tails.

MARYLAND

6. Delmarva Fox Squirrel

The Delmarva fox squirrel is one of Maryland's endangered species. This large tree squirrel is shy and quiet. It is not very good at climbing trees, and it usually runs along the ground when chased by a predator. It has a gray body and a fluffy tail that can grow to 15 inches (38 cm) long.

7. Great Blue Heron

The great blue heron is the largest kind of heron found in North America. It is blue-gray with a black stripe over its eye. The great blue heron can be found along Maryland's marshes, ponds, and lakes. It uses its large pointed bill to catch fish.

8. Osprey

About a quarter of America's osprey make the Chesapeake Bay their home during the spring and summer. They feed on the abundant fish in the bay. Their nests can be seen in trees, on telephone poles, and other high places.

9. River Otter

The river otter is the only otter found in Maryland. This whiskered mammal likes to make its home on riversides throughout the state. Its eyes have adapted to swimming underwater. River otters have trouble seeing above water.

10. State Tree: White Oak

The white oak is named for its white-colored bark and gray twigs. It grows to a height of 60 to 150 feet (18–46 m). The white oak has bright, glossy leaves. Native Americans used to ground the tree's acorns into flour, and the white oak's wood is used for lumber.

Delmarva Fox Squirrel

Great Blue Heron

River Otter

This illustration is depicting surveyors laying out the town of Baltimore after its founding in 1729.

From the Beginning

Maryland is the most southern of the Middle Atlantic States. It shares features of both the North and the South. Its people have had divided loyalties going back as far as the American Revolution. Different groups of people in the state were loyal to different causes. Marylanders have usually met history's challenges with courage and determination.

The First Peoples of Maryland

Native Americans first came to Maryland around 10,000 BCE. The only hints to their cultures are artifacts such as pottery, arrowheads, and burial sites.

By the 1600s, various Algonquian-speaking tribes were living along the Chesapeake Bay. The Piscataway and Patuxent peoples lived west of the bay. The Choptank, Nanticoke, and Assateague lived on the Eastern Shore. The Iroquois-speaking Susquehannock settled in the north at the head of the bay. Some lived in long huts. Others preferred oval wigwams made from wood and covered with bark or matting. Villages were small and consisted of only several hundred people. The men hunted, fished, and gathered shellfish from the bay. The women grew corn, squash, beans, and tobacco. Many tribes moved inland for the winter. However, European newcomers would soon challenge this way of life.

The arrival of European explorers and settlers greatly changed the way of life of Maryland's Native Americans.

Explorers and Settlers

Italian explorer Giovanni da Verrazzano may have been the first European to see Maryland. He sailed past the Chesapeake Bay in 1524 while exploring the shoreline of America for the king of France. The first explorer to actually visit the area was Englishman John Smith. In 1608, Smith sailed up the Chesapeake Bay. He described the area that would become Maryland as a "fruitful and delightsome land!"

However, Smith decided to return to the Jamestown colony in Virginia. In 1607, he had helped found the colony, the first permanent English settlement in America. William Claiborne, another member of the Virginia colony, also began exploring to the north. He was attracted to the Chesapeake Bay and saw its potential for colonization. Claiborne set up a trading post on Kent Island in the bay in 1631. That was the first permanent European settlement in present-day Maryland.

The next year, King Charles I of England granted the region to George Calvert, the first Lord Baltimore. At the time, many European Protestants and Catholics did not get along. In England, where the rulers were Protestant, laws punished people who practiced Catholicism. England's American colonies had similar laws. Calvert wanted Maryland to be a safe place for Catholics to settle. Calvert died later in 1632, and his son Cecilius Calvert received the land grant. He named the colony Maryland after Charles I's wife, Queen Henrietta Maria, whom the English often called Queen Mary. In March 1634, Cecilius's brother Leonard landed in Maryland with two ships carrying settlers, the *Ark* and the *Dove*. He founded the settlement of St. Mary's City in Southern Maryland. The city became the first capital of the colony.

In 1649, the **legislature** passed the Act Concerning Religion, which gave all Christians living in Maryland the right to choose how they worshipped. Passed to protect the Catholic minority, it is one of the first laws granting religious freedom in America.

This painting shows Leonard Calvert planting a cross to mark the settlement of St. Mary's City in 1634.

The Native People

Maryland is a small but geographically diverse state. The Native tribes that lived in the region at the time of the European settlement were distributed along those geographic lines. When the *Ark* and the *Dove* landed at what is now St. Mary's City in Southern Maryland, they encountered members of a Powhatan tribe. Chief Powhatan united many tribes into a confederacy. The Nanticoke, including the Piscataway and the Conoy, dominated the Eastern Shore. The Lenape lived in the northeast corner that today borders Pennsylvania and Delaware. The Susquehannock populated the hilly region north of present-day Baltimore, and the Tutelo and Sapolo were found in the parts of the Piedmont Plateau that now include Montgomery, Howard, and Frederick counties. The Ohio Valley tribes, including the Shawnee, lived in mountainous Western Maryland.

The Native people throughout Maryland had different customs, but in many ways, their daily lives had striking similarities. Most Natives in the area lived in longhouses or wigwams. They hunted, grew crops such as corn, beans, and squash, and fished the abundant waters. They made their clothing from animal skins and grasses.

As had happened in many other parts of the United States, Europeans coming into contact with the Natives led to the tribes of Maryland contracting several epidemic diseases, including smallpox, measles, and **tuberculosis**. Without immunity built up, the illnesses proved deadly, wiping out thousands of Natives. The colonial expansion of Maryland drove out most of the rest of the Native people during the 1700s. Many were forced to move to reservations in Oklahoma and Kansas. These tribes still exist, but for the most part do not live in Maryland.

Today there are more than 20,000 Native Americans in the state, but there are no federally recognized tribes in Maryland. On January 9, 2012, Governor Martin O'Malley signed two executive orders making the Piscataway Indian Nation and the Piscataway Conoy Tribe the first tribes ever recognized by the state.

Spotlight on the Piscataway

The Piscataway tribe is an Algonquian-speaking tribe that lived, and continues to live, along the Chesapeake Bay in Maryland. "Piscataway" means "where the waters blend." The Piscataway were one of the largest tribes in Maryland; however, after Europeans colonized the area, the population decreased.

Shown here is an Algonquian longhouse similar to what the Piscataway tribe lived in.

Homes: Like many other Algonquian tribes, the Piscataway lived in longhouses. Longhouses were long and rectangular, and were of various lengths. The roofs were often barrel-shaped, and they were covered with bark or woven mats.

Trade: Trade was a very important aspect of Piscataway culture. The tribe often traded tools, food, and weapons with other Native American tribes. After the Europeans arrived in the 17th century, the tribe traded what they had with the Europeans for metal and firearms.

Art: The Piscataway people were talented potters, but their pottery had a more practical purpose. They used pottery to store food and to protect their seeds before planting.

Dance: The Rabbit Dance was a dance that took place at Piscataway social dances. The Rabbit Dance called for the women to choose a male dance partner. According to legend, if a man refused, he would turn into a rabbit!

The Ring Dance, or Hoop Dance, featured a dancer who picked up one hoop at a time, each hoop completing a new symbol of nature, such as a turtle, eagle, or the world.

Visitors can learn about colonial Maryland at the Thomas Stone National Historic Site, a restored plantation from the 1770s.

A Growing Colony

The Calvert family ruled the Maryland colony despite several disputes, including a **feud** with Claiborne over Kent Island. In 1689, colonists seized the government and demanded that the king take over the colony. The first royal governor arrived in 1692. Two years later, the capital was moved from St. Mary's City to Anne Arundel Town. Later, its name would be changed to Annapolis.

Maryland farmers started tobacco plantations along the rivers that empty into the Chesapeake Bay. They needed many workers for these big farms. Africans were first brought to Maryland by ship in the 1600s. Then, in 1664, slavery—the enslavement of blacks for life—became legal in the colony. But before the 1700s, both black and white indentured servants were more common than slaves. Indentured servants were people whose passage to America was paid in exchange for work for a master, usually for up to seven years. After that period, the servant was freed. Mathias de Sousa was a black indentured servant who arrived with the first colonists in 1634. He soon gained his freedom and in 1642, he became the first black man to serve in the state's general assembly.

By the 1700s, African slaves had replaced most white indentured servants on the large tobacco **plantations**. Most of the slaves led miserable lives. They were forced to work long hours six days a week and they were housed in shabby cabins.

The colony continued to grow. During the 1700s, European settlers forced many Native Americans to move west, out of Maryland. Some Native Americans were killed when they refused to give up their land. Others died of diseases brought by the settlers from Europe. Today, only about 5,000 Native Americans live in the state.

The city of Baltimore, founded in 1729, became a center where farmers could sell their goods. In the 1760s, Maryland quarreled with Pennsylvania over its border. That **dispute** included Pennsylvania's three lower counties, which are now the state of Delaware. The British government sent Charles Mason and a surveyor, Jeremiah Dixon, to mark the boundary line between the two colonies. A surveyor is a person who measures the size and position of a piece of land. Completed in 1767, their survey was used less than a decade later to separate the states of Maryland, Delaware, and Pennsylvania. In the 1800s, the Mason-Dixon Line became a symbolic border between Northern "free" and Southern slave states.

The American Revolution

A larger conflict was growing between Great Britain and its American colonies. While tobacco farmers and some other Marylanders were on good terms with the British, many colonists wanted independence. In 1774, Maryland patriots in Annapolis copied the Boston Tea Party of 1773. They protested the British tax on tea by burning a British ship, the *Peggy Stewart*, and its cargo of tea.

Making a Fruit Bird Feeder

Baltimore orioles love to eat fruit. This feeder will help attract them to your house. If orioles do not live in your area, this feeder will help attract other birds that eat fruit, such as catbirds, robins, and tanagers.

What You Need

A clean, empty plastic jug, such as a fruit juice container

Wooden sticks

Colorful yarn or string

Orange

1 cup (240 ml) grape jelly

Knife

Safety scissors

What To Do

- Have an adult cut out two large rectangles on both sides of the jug, several inches from the bottom. The openings should be big enough for a small bird to reach the bottom of the jug.
- Have an adult make small slits in the bottle with the knife where the sticks will go through the bottle. There will be a total of 6 slits (2 on the top for the orange, 2 below the orange for the birds to perch on, and 2 below the rectangular openings).
- Push the sticks through these openings. Trim with scissors if necessary.

- Tie your yarn in a knot making a loop. Make it long enough to hang.
- Put the yarn over the opening of the jug and tighten the cap back over the yarn.
- Cut the orange in half and place on each side of the top stick.
- Fill the bottom of the feeder with jelly.
- Hang the feeder outside from a tree or bird feeder stand.
- Enjoy watching the birds!

War broke out in April 1775. Not much fighting took place in Maryland during the American Revolution. Maryland soldiers, however, fought bravely in many battles.

The colonists won their independence in 1783. The Thirteen Colonies—now states—struggled to find a new form of government. In September 1786, Annapolis hosted a states' convention. **Delegates** discussed the issues of trade and business. They agreed to meet again in Philadelphia in 1787.

At the Philadelphia convention, delegates wrote the U.S. Constitution. It was a bold plan for a national government. On April 28, 1788, Maryland became the seventh state to ratify, or approve, the new Constitution.

"The Second American Revolution"

In 1812, the United States once again went to war with Great Britain. People sometimes call the War of 1812 the second American Revolution. This time a good deal of fighting took place in Maryland. In 1813, the British entered the Chesapeake Bay, attacking ships and raiding towns. In September 1814, one month after British forces burned much of Washington, D.C., they attacked Baltimore. American lawyer Francis Scott Key was aboard a **truce** boat, awaiting the release of an American doctor imprisoned by the British.

This painting shows the burning of the *Peggy Stewart* by Maryland colonists in October 1774.

This painting from the 1800s shows a woman who symbolizes America holding the American flag, or star-spangled banner.

From the boat, he watched the British bombard Fort McHenry, which guards the entrance to Baltimore harbor. All day and into the night on September 13, Key watched British ships fire rockets and exploding bombs at the fort.

To Key's joy, the next morning the American flag still flew over the fort "by the dawn's early light." The British retreated. Key began to write a poem about the event, which he finished that night. Less than a week later, his poem, "Defense of Fort McHenry," was published in a Baltimore newspaper. It was later set to the tune of an English song and became "The Star-Spangled Banner." In 1931, 88 years after Key's death, his patriotic song officially became the U.S. national anthem.

The United States and Great Britain signed a peace treaty ending the War of 1812 in December 1814. (Because news traveled slowly at that time, a major American victory in the war, at the Battle of New Orleans, actually took place in January 1815.)

The Civil War

Maryland made great strides in the 1800s in industry and development. The first national highway, called the National Road, was finished in 1818. It joined Cumberland, Maryland, with Wheeling, Virginia (now in West Virginia). Peter Cooper built one of the first American steam locomotives, *Tom Thumb*. The locomotive made its first run on the new Baltimore & Ohio Railroad in 1830. In 1844, Samuel Morse sent the first message over a telegraph line from Washington, D.C., to Baltimore.

Civil Rights Pioneer

Frederick Douglass was born a slave on a plantation in Talbot County, Maryland. As a servant in Baltimore, he was taught the alphabet, and he taught himself to read and write. Douglass escaped to freedom in Massachusetts, where he spoke out against slavery. His autobiography shared the plight of slaves with readers.

The LaVale Toll Gate House in LaVale, Maryland, was built along the National Road in the 1830s.

10 KEY CITIES

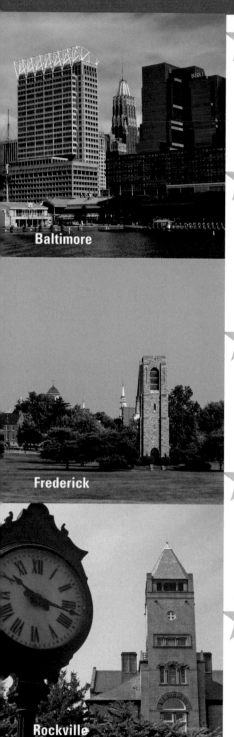

Baltimore

Frederick

Rockville

1. Baltimore: population 620,961

Nicknamed "Charm City," Baltimore is Maryland's largest city. It is also known as the "city of neighborhoods" because of its numerous districts, such as the Inner Harbor. Baltimore is known for its science and health industries.

2. Frederick: population 65,239

Frederick, in Central Maryland, is an 18th century town known for its shops, galleries, restaurants, and antique stores. Visitors also enjoy nearby Civil War tourist destinations, such as the Antietam and Gettysburg Battlefields and the National Museum of Civil War Medicine.

3. Rockville: population 61,209

Located northwest of Washington, D.C., Rockville is part of the Baltimore-Washington Metropolitan Area. The Rockville area is home to many software and biotechnology companies. The city offers theater, shopping, and dining.

4. Gaithersburg: population 59,933

Gaithersburg has two main areas. Olde Town is a historic district on the east side of town, which includes businesses and landmarks. The west side of town has more modern businesses, shopping, and wealthy neighborhoods.

5. Bowie: population 54,727

Bowie, located between Baltimore and Washington, D.C., has more than 1,100 acres (445 ha) of parks and preserved open space. This includes more than 22 miles (35 km) of trails that residents and visitors can walk.

MARYLAND ★ ★ ★

6. Hagerstown: population 39,662

Hagerstown, in West-Central Maryland, has a lot of cultural attractions, such as the Maryland Theatre, Maryland Symphony Orchestra, and the Washington County Museum of Fine Arts. Hagerstown is home to the Western Maryland Blues Fest.

7. Annapolis: population 38,394

On the bank of the Chesapeake Bay is Annapolis, the capital of Maryland. Annapolis is a very historically important city. It was the first peacetime capital of the United States, from 1783 to 1784. Congress ratified the Treaty of Paris in Annapolis, which ended the American Revolution.

8. College Park: population 30,413

Home to the University of Maryland, College Park, this city is just minutes from Washington, D.C. Half of the city's residents are students, but many people who work in Washington live in this bustling suburb.

9. Salisbury: population 30,343

Nicknamed "the crossroads of Delmarva," Salisbury is the commercial center of the Delmarva Peninsula, part of which Maryland occupies, along with Delaware and Virginia. It is the largest city on the Eastern Shore, and it is popular for its proximity to the Chesapeake Bay and the Atlantic Ocean.

10. Laurel: population 25,115

Laurel is a small city that is home to many people who work in nearby Washington, D.C. and Baltimore. Laurel has small theaters, parks, and year-round festivals, including a street fair along the city's main street.

Annapolis

College Park

This illustration shows slaves escaping from Maryland to Delaware by way of the Underground Railroad.

All these achievements helped bring Americans closer together, but the issue of slavery moved them farther apart. By the mid–1800s, most people in the North opposed slavery. In the South, most people supported it. Harriet Tubman, a runaway slave from Maryland, helped many other slaves escape from the South. She was the most famous "conductor" on the Underground Railroad, a network of secret routes and people who helped slaves travel from one "station," or safe hiding place, to another on their way to freedom in the North.

By early 1861, a number of Southern states had seceded, or broken away, from the United States, or Union. They formed the Confederate States of America. The people of Maryland were torn. Many wanted Maryland to remain in the Union, and it did. Yet some still relied on slave labor, and many sided with the Confederacy. On April 19 in Baltimore, a mob of pro-Confederates attacked troops from Massachusetts who were traveling to Washington, D.C. Four soldiers and twelve other people died in the riot. They were the first people killed in the Civil War. (The first shots of the war had been fired a week earlier when Confederate forces attacked Fort Sumter in South Carolina).

More than 70,000 Maryland soldiers fought in the war. About 50,000 of them fought for the Union. Several important battles were fought in the state. The biggest was the Battle of Antietam on September 17, 1862.

Confederate General Robert E. Lee had invaded Maryland with 37,400 troops two weeks earlier. Under General George McClellan, 56,000 Union soldiers met them at Antietam Creek near Sharpsburg. The fighting began in the early morning and continued throughout the day. When the battle ended—with a Union victory—more than 23,000 soldiers on both sides were wounded or dead. It was the bloodiest one-day battle of the Civil War.

After Antietam, Lee retreated to Virginia. The Union victory gave President Abraham Lincoln the opportunity to issue an early version of his Emancipation Proclamation. In the final proclamation, effective January 1, 1863, Lincoln declared that all slaves in Confederate-controlled territory "shall be then, thenceforward, and forever free."

In 1864, Maryland adopted a new state constitution that **abolished** slavery. It also denied Confederate supporters the right to vote. The war ended in Union victory the following year. In December 1865, the Thirteenth Amendment to the U.S. Constitution officially ended slavery throughout the United States.

Growth and Reform

In the years following the Civil War, Maryland became a leader in science and education. Johns Hopkins University was founded in Baltimore in 1876. The world-famous Johns Hopkins Hospital opened thirteen years later. Today, the hospital and school remain important research centers. Johns Hopkins doctors have discovered new treatments for **tuberculosis** and other diseases. In 1886, Baltimore established one of the first free public library systems in the country.

Maryland at War

The United States entered World War I in 1917. More than 62,000 Marylanders served in the armed forces. The U.S. Army established Aberdeen Proving Ground near the Chesapeake Bay in 1917 to test new weapons. Today, it is the oldest active proving ground. In Anne Arundel County, the War Department established a base that became known as Fort Meade. During the war, more than 400,000 soldiers passed through Fort Meade, which remains a major Army base today.

Police agents near Waldorf, Maryland take control of illegal equipment used to make alcohol during Prohibition in 1925.

Prohibition

In 1919, the Eighteenth Amendment to the U.S. Constitution banned the manufacture, sale, and transportation of alcoholic beverages throughout the country. The period when alcohol was illegal is called Prohibition. The Maryland state government did not want the federal government telling Marylanders what to do. (Prohibition was not very popular with many Americans and was repealed by another constitutional amendment in 1933.) During Prohibition, Marylanders were encouraged to defy the law by their own governor, Albert C. Ritchie. Legend has it that this fierce independence earned Maryland the nickname the Free State.

Depression and More War

During the 1930s, the Great Depression caused great hardship for Marylanders and people across the country. Thousands of banks failed, businesses closed, and millions of people were out of work. The U.S. government created many new programs to help the nation recover. In Maryland, the government built a new town, called Greenbelt, not far from Washington, D.C. Building the town created new jobs and gave people affordable places to live.

On December 7, 1941, the Japanese bombed the U.S. naval base in Pearl Harbor, Hawaii. The USS *Maryland*, named after the state, was one of the battleships damaged in the attack. The next day, the United States entered World War II. During the war, some 55,000 Marylanders served in the armed forces. Many more worked in shipbuilding, aircraft manufacturing, and other wartime industries. Women took over the jobs of many men who were called to fight overseas. After the war ended in 1945, the state had more jobs than people to fill them. Maryland's cities and towns grew bigger than ever. From 1940 to 1950, the state's population grew by more than 500,000.

The Civil War in Maryland

Seven battles were fought in Maryland from 1862 to 1864. All took place in the western part of the state. More people died at Antietam than during the other six battles combined.

Women work as welders in a Maryland steel mill during World War II.

Thurgood Marshall was one of the most important figures in the fight for civil rights.

Camp David

Located in a quiet wooded area of Western Maryland, Camp David is the official "retreat" of the president of the United States—a place where the president can go to relax and to work away from the bustle of Washington, D.C. President Franklin D. Roosevelt first used the retreat in 1942. It was given the name Camp David in the 1950s by President Dwight D. Eisenhower, in honor of his grandson David.

Struggle for Freedom

Despite the state's growing prosperity, many African Americans felt left behind. Like many other states, Maryland had laws that forced blacks and whites to use separate public facilities, such as train cars, restaurants, and schools. In this system of separation, or segregation, the quality of services offered to blacks was not as good as what was offered to whites. Maryland's African Americans had long been fighting to gain the same treatment as whites. The National Association for the Advancement of Colored People (NAACP) is an organization that fights for civil rights. The NAACP's second-oldest chapter had been founded in Baltimore in 1913. Baltimore is now the organization's home.

NAACP attorney Thurgood Marshall, from Baltimore, was a leader in the fight for civil rights. In 1954, he won a U.S. Supreme Court decision against segregation in public schools. In 1967, President Lyndon Johnson appointed Marshall to the U.S. Supreme Court. He was the first African American to receive that honor. Marshall served on the Court for 24 years before retiring in 1991 at age 83.

Though African Americans had made gains in racial equality, their struggle was far from over. Civil rights leader Martin Luther King Jr. was assassinated in Memphis, Tennessee, in 1968. His murder led to riots in Baltimore and other U.S. cities. The riots had a lasting negative effect on Baltimore, which was already struggling. The city's population had peaked in the years after World War II. In 1950, Baltimore was the sixth-largest city in the United States. But as large numbers of white people moved to neighboring areas, or suburbs, the population began to fall.

As suburbs **prospered**, Baltimore began to suffer. Many African Americans either could not afford to move to suburbs or were not allowed to because of discrimination. The manufacturing jobs that had been so vital to the city's economy disappeared.

The economy of the whole state suffered in the 1970s. Many businesses closed or moved to other states, leaving thousands of Marylanders out of work.

Baltimore's Inner Harbor area is one of the biggest tourist attractions in the state.

Rebuilding Baltimore

In the 1970s, the government took steps to attract businesses and tourism to Baltimore. In the mid–1970s, the city celebrated the opening of the Baltimore

Convention Center and the Baltimore World Trade Center—at 400 feet (123m), it's the tallest building with five even sides (pentagon) in the world. In 1980, a new business area called Harborplace opened in what had become a run-down area of the old harbor (or Inner Harbor) in Baltimore. Tourists flocked to its shops and restaurants. The National Aquarium opened in the Inner Harbor district the following year. In the 1990s, the city built new stadiums for its baseball team, the Orioles, and its new professional football team, the Ravens. But even as tourism increased, the city's population continued to fall. In 2010, Baltimore ranked twentieth in the nation.

Maryland Today

Today, Maryland is home to many high-tech industries. Light technology such as computers, lab work, and scientific research has replaced heavy industry in its cities. The federal government has many scientific agencies that are headquartered in Maryland. The National Institute of Health in Bethesda performs medical research. Scientists and engineers at the Goddard Space Flight Center in Greenbelt develop new instruments and technology to study Earth and outer space. The Old Line State has moved into the twenty-first century with renewed confidence.

The visitor center at the Goddard Space Flight Center has popular exhibits about the study and exploration of space.

10 KEY DATES IN STATE HISTORY

1. June-July, 1608

Englishman John Smith explores Chesapeake Bay and maps it. When he returns to England, his maps and journals describing the Chesapeake Bay are published.

2. Spring 1631

William Claiborne founds the first permanent European settlement in what is now Maryland, on Kent Island. Claiborne turns his trading post into a plantation. By the late 1630s, there are more than 100 people living there.

3. July 30, 1729

Baltimore is founded. It is named after Lord Baltimore, the first Governor of the Province of Maryland.

4. April 28, 1788

Maryland ratifies the U.S. Constitution and becomes the seventh state. Two years later, Maryland donates land that becomes the nation's capital, Washington, D.C.

5. September 12-14, 1814

The British attack Maryland during the War of 1812. American soldiers defend Baltimore in September, inspiring Francis Scott Key to write a poem that would become the lyrics to "The Star-Spangled Banner."

6. September 17, 1862

The Union Army wins the Battle of Antietam in Sharpsburg. More than 23,000 soldiers are wounded or killed. The battle ends the Confederate Army's first invasion of the north during the Civil War.

7. June 1, 1967

Marylander Thurgood Marshall is appointed to the U.S. Supreme Court. He becomes the first African American U.S. Supreme Court Justice.

8. January 28, 2001

The Baltimore Ravens win their first Super Bowl. The team would go on to win another Super Bowl in 2013.

9. 2008

Maryland native Michael Phelps wins a record eight gold medals at the Olympics in Beijing, China. After the 2012 Summer Olympics, Phelps becomes the most decorated athlete in modern Olympic history.

10. May 2, 2013

Maryland becomes the 18th state to abolish the death penalty. The law replaces the death penalty with a sentence to life without the possibility of parole.

A young girl enjoys a Maryland beach.

The People

Maryland's residents come from a wide range of cultures. Many share heritages brought by their European **ancestors**. These include the Irish, Germans, English, Italians, and Polish. People with roots in India, Mexico, China, and other Asian and Latin American nations celebrate their own rich cultures. Some have lived in Maryland all their lives, while others are new to the state. No matter how long people have lived in the state, the blending of their cultures, beliefs, and abilities has helped make Maryland a unique place to live and work.

Many businesses that specialize in ethnic foods and other goods bring an international flavor to Maryland. Langley Park near Washington, D.C., is one of the many cities that have growing Hispanic communities. In places like these, American traditions are mixed with cultures from the Caribbean and from Mexico, Central America, and South America. Across the state, festivals and other cultural celebrations are also held throughout the year. Baltimore alone hosts the Polish Festival, LatinoFest, Fest Africa, India Festival, and more.

A Native American dancer performs at the Healing Horse Spirit Powwow in Mount Airy.

Native Americans

Before the Europeans arrived, there were more than 20 Native American groups on the land that is now Maryland. Many tribes were forced to move as Europeans began to settle in the area. Today, less than one percent of Maryland's population is Native American.

Before the American colonies were established, the Accohannock Tribe lived on the eastern shores of Maryland and Virginia. The tribe is currently trying to obtain federal recognition. Such recognition would enable the tribe to claim a legal relationship to the U.S. government and receive federal aid.

Every year, the tribe holds the Native American Heritage Festival and Powwow. At this event, the Accohannocks celebrate their traditions and culture. Members of the tribe also attend powwows in other states and present their culture to schools and other organizations.

African Americans

African Americans are Maryland's largest minority. They make up about 29 percent of the population. In Baltimore, nearly two-thirds of the residents are black.

A number of African Americans have moved from Washington, D.C., to nearby Prince George's County in southeastern Maryland. Once mostly white, Prince George's County is now more than 65 percent black. Wayne K. Curry was the first African American to hold the county's executive position. He served from 1994 to 2002.

Did You Know?

Clara Barton National Historic Site commemorates Clara Barton, who is the founder of the American Red Cross. The house, located in Glen Echo, was her home, the headquarters for the American Red Cross, and a warehouse for supplies.

People of all races make Maryland their home.

10 KEY PEOPLE

Benjamin Banneker

Anna Faris

Billie Holiday

1. Carmelo Anthony

Carmelo Anthony was born in Brooklyn in 1984, but raised in Baltimore. Anthony's mother pushed him to play sports and focus on school. Anthony played basketball at Syracuse University, and he led the team to the NCAA Tournament championship in 2003. Since then, Anthony has played for the Denver Nuggets and the New York Knicks.

2. Benjamin Banneker

Born in Baltimore in 1731, Benjamin Banneker was an African American farmer, mathematician, astronomer, and a surveyor. He helped Thomas Jefferson survey the new capital in Washington, D.C.

3. Anna Faris

Born in Baltimore in 1976, Anna Faris started acting in plays as a child. After graduating from college, she got her big break when she starred in the *Scary Movie* series. Faris is best known for her roles in comedies, such as the *The House Bunny* and *Cloudy with a Chance of Meatballs*.

4. Billie Holiday

Billie Holiday was one of America's great jazz singers. Born in Philadelphia in 1915, she was raised in Baltimore. At 18, Holiday made her first record. Musicians respected her ability to express the pain and loneliness in her life through her singing.

5. Michael Phelps

Born in Baltimore in 1985, Michael Phelps learned to swim at the North Baltimore Aquatic Club. He swam in his first Olympics in 2000 when he was just 15. In 2012, Phelps won his 22nd medal.

6. Edgar Allen Poe

Edgar Allan Poe was born in Boston in 1809, but he lived with his wife in Maryland and is buried in Baltimore. He wrote poetry and horror stories. Baltimore's professional football team, the Ravens, is named after his most famous poem, "The Raven."

7. Nora Roberts

Born in Silver Spring in 1950, Nora Roberts never dreamed she would become a famous writer. After getting snowed in with her two sons, Roberts tried a new activity to keep her busy: writing. She sold her first book in 1981, and since then, Roberts has written more than 200 novels.

8. Babe Ruth

Born in Baltimore in 1895, George Herman "Babe" Ruth was the first great home-run hitter. Playing for the New York Yankees, he hit 60 home runs in 1927. This record was not broken until 1961. Ruth hit a total of 714 home runs in his career.

9. Jada Pinkett Smith

Born in Baltimore in 1971, Smith was a performer from a young age. She attended the Baltimore School for the Arts, and moved to Los Angeles. Smith landed a part on the TV show *A Different World*. Since then, Smith has appeared in *The Nutty Professor* and *The Matrix Revolutions*.

10. Harriet Tubman

Harriet Tubman was born into slavery in Maryland in the early 1800s. After escaping to the North, she was part of the Underground Railroad, and she helped many other runaway slaves. After the Civil War, she settled in New York, where she fought for women's rights.

Nora Roberts

Babe Ruth

Jada Pinkett Smith

Who Marylanders Are

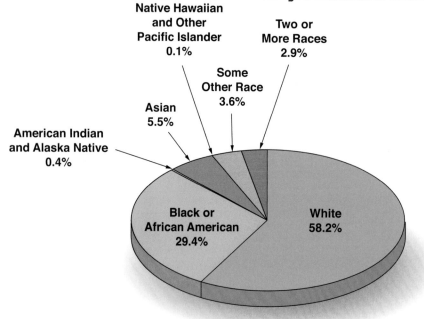

Native Hawaiian and Other Pacific Islander 0.1%

Two or More Races 2.9%

Some Other Race 3.6%

Asian 5.5%

American Indian and Alaska Native 0.4%

Black or African American 29.4%

White 58.2%

Total Population 5,773,552

Hispanic or Latino (of any race):

• 470,632 people (8.2%)

Note: The pie chart shows the racial breakdown of the state's population based on the categories used by the U.S. Bureau of the Census. The Census Bureau reports information for Hispanics or Latinos separately, since they may be of any race. Percentages in the pie chart may not add to 100 because of rounding.

Source: U.S. Bureau of the Census, 2010 Census

In 2003, Michael Steele became Maryland's lieutenant governor. That is the second-highest office in the state government. Steele was the first African American to be elected to a statewide office in Maryland. He is a member of the Republican Party—one of the two main political parties in the United States. (The other is the Democratic Party.) In 2009, Steele became the first African American to chair the Republican National Committee, which sets the party's platform or goals and raises money.

City of Neighborhoods, Museums, and Music

About nine of every ten Marylanders live in or near a city. The rest live in rural areas. Annapolis, the state capital, is small. It has only about 38,000 people. Baltimore is the state's largest city, with a population of almost 621,000.

Baltimore is known as the city of neighborhoods. Many of those neighborhoods were formed in the 1800s by European immigrants who wanted to live near people from their homelands. They wanted to be able to speak their native languages and help each other find jobs and places to live. Today, there are more than 225 neighborhoods in the city.

Many Irish people once lived in southwestern Baltimore. They helped build the Baltimore & Ohio Railroad. The houses they once lived in were supposed to be torn down. However, local residents worked to restore them. The railroad's old engine roundhouse nearby has been turned into a museum. A roundhouse is a circular building that is used for storing and repairing locomotives.

Another museum in Baltimore is dedicated to African Americans. The National Great Blacks in Wax Museum has more than a hundred life-size wax figures of famous Maryland African Americans. One of the figures is of Matthew Henson. In 1909, he was among the first explorers to reach the North Pole, as part of an expedition led by Robert Peary. The museum also has a large model of a slave ship.

Downtown Baltimore has many things to see, such as Harborplace and Camden Yards, the home of the Orioles baseball team. The National Aquarium is seven stories high and has an Atlantic coral reef with 335,000 gallons (1.3 million liters) of water and hundreds of tropical reef fish. Visitors can also walk through a South American rain forest encased in glass or explore an Australian Outback river gorge.

Music lovers may enjoy the Baltimore Symphony Orchestra, which plays classical music. Fans of jazz can see live performances at the Eubie Blake National Jazz Institute and Cultural Center. Eubie Blake was a famous ragtime and jazz composer who was popular in the early twentieth century.

Young Baltimore Orioles fans check out the field at Camden Yards before a game.

A Leader in Education

Education is important in Maryland. One of the first U.S. public high schools opened in Baltimore in 1839. Western High School, which opened in 1844, is the oldest all-girls public high school in the country. There are more than 1,400 public schools and more than 1,200 private schools throughout the state. Since 2003, Maryland has funded charter schools as well. Charter schools are public schools (tax-supported) run by independent groups rather than local school boards. They have specific educational goals. In 2012, a higher percentage of Maryland high school students passed their Advanced Placement (AP) exams than in any other state. Students who pass AP exams can earn credit toward a college degree.

More than one in three adult Marylanders is a college graduate. That is one of the highest percentages in the nation. Today, college-bound students can choose from more than a dozen universities in Maryland. Since 1999, students have been able to take college courses on the Internet.

George Washington helped found the first college in the state in 1782. It is called Washington College in his honor. Mount St. Mary's in Emmitsburg is the country's second-oldest Catholic college. The University of Maryland in College Park is the largest college in the state, with more than 37,000 students. It was founded on a former plantation in 1859. The University of Maryland, Baltimore County, is one of the most diverse colleges in the country. A large percentage of its students are either Asian American or African American. Annapolis is the home of the U.S. Naval Academy. Cadets spend their summers training on ships at sea. When they graduate, cadets become officers in the U.S. Navy or the Marine Corps.

Sports and Recreation

Marylanders like to work and study, but they also like to play. The state is home to the Baltimore Orioles baseball team and the Baltimore Ravens football team. The Redskins football team may be from Washington, D.C., but the team plays its home games in Landover, Maryland. A half-dozen minor league baseball teams are also based in the state, from the Hagerstown Suns to the Delmarva Shorebirds in Salisbury.

Horse racing has been a tradition at Pimlico Race Course in Baltimore since 1870. The first Preakness Stakes was held three years later. Tens of thousands of fans still crowd the stands and the track's grassy infield to watch the Preakness. It is the second race of horse racing's Triple Crown series.

Annapolis's beautiful harbor is one of the top centers for sailing on the East Coast. Visitors can sail aboard the schooner *Woodwind*, a replica, or copy, of a luxury yacht from the early 1900s. During their tour of the harbor, amateur sailors can help the crew raise the sails and even take turns steering the ship.

One of the state's most popular sports—lacrosse—is the oldest team sport in North America. It was invented by Native Americans. Each player uses a stick with a net attached at one end to throw a ball into the opposite team's goal. Johns Hopkins University, the University of Maryland, Baltimore County, the University of Maryland, College Park, and Loyola College have some of the best men's college lacrosse teams. The powerhouse University of Maryland Lady Terrapins have won more lacrosse national championships than any other team.

Maryland's state sport is jousting. This sport was developed in the Middle Ages when knights on horseback tried to knock each other to the ground with long metal-tipped wooden spears called lances. Marylanders have enjoyed jousting since colonial times. They play a less violent form of jousting. Riders attempt to "spear" hanging rings with a lance. Each rider must do this while galloping on horseback. The one who lifts the most rings is the champion.

First-year students at the U.S. Naval Academy in Annapolis take part in a demanding training experience.

10 KEY EVENTS ★

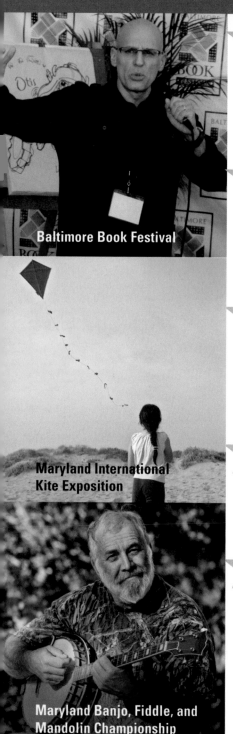

Baltimore Book Festival

Maryland International Kite Exposition

Maryland Banjo, Fiddle, and Mandolin Championship

1. African American Festival

Held in the summer, Baltimore's African American Festival is a celebration of African American life, culture, and music. More than 500,000 people attend the festival, and they enjoy food, performances, art, and seminars.

2. Baltimore Book Festival

The Baltimore Book Festival is a celebration of the literary world that's held every September. Readings, book signings, discussions, and workshops are just some of the events that take place there.

3. Festival of Trees

The Festival of Trees is one of the largest holiday festivals in the Northeast. This three-day event, in Timonium, features more than five hundred decorated holiday trees, gingerbread houses, crafts, and entertainment for the whole family.

4. Maryland International Kite Exposition

This weekend event is held in April in Ocean City. It features kites of all kinds, colors, and sizes. Among the many contests are a stunt kite championship and a kite makers' competition.

5. Maryland State Banjo, Fiddle, and Mandolin Championship

Held in Oakland in the fall, this two-day, friendly competition features musicians playing country and bluegrass music. Musicians of all ages compete for cash prizes and the state title.

MARYLAND ★ ★ ★ ★

6. Maryland State Fair

For eleven days in August, Timonium hosts the state fair, which includes livestock shows, rides, arts and crafts, music, horse racing, and contests. At the birthing center, visitors can see local farmers' cows and pigs give birth to their young.

7. National Hard Crab Derby and Fair

This September celebration in Crisfield includes crab-picking and crab-cooking contests, a plastic boat regatta, and the crab derby. More than four hundred crabs with numbered shells race each other. There are also rides, food, crafts, and games.

8. Preakness Celebration

The Preakness Stakes is held every May at Pimlico Race Course in Baltimore. It is one of the most famous horse races in the country. The Preakness Celebration includes parades, concerts, and fireworks.

9. Skipjack Race and Festival

During Labor Day weekend, many people gather on Deal Island for this event. Activities include arts and crafts, contests, and the annual skipjack races—which honor the official state boat. A skipjack is a small boat with one mast and a V-shaped bottom.

10. Sunfest

Sunfest, held in September, is one of Maryland's most popular festivals. Taking place in Ocean City, this festival features performers, art, music, and food. There are also activities for children, such as pumpkin decorating and hayrides.

Maryland State Fair

Preakness Celebration

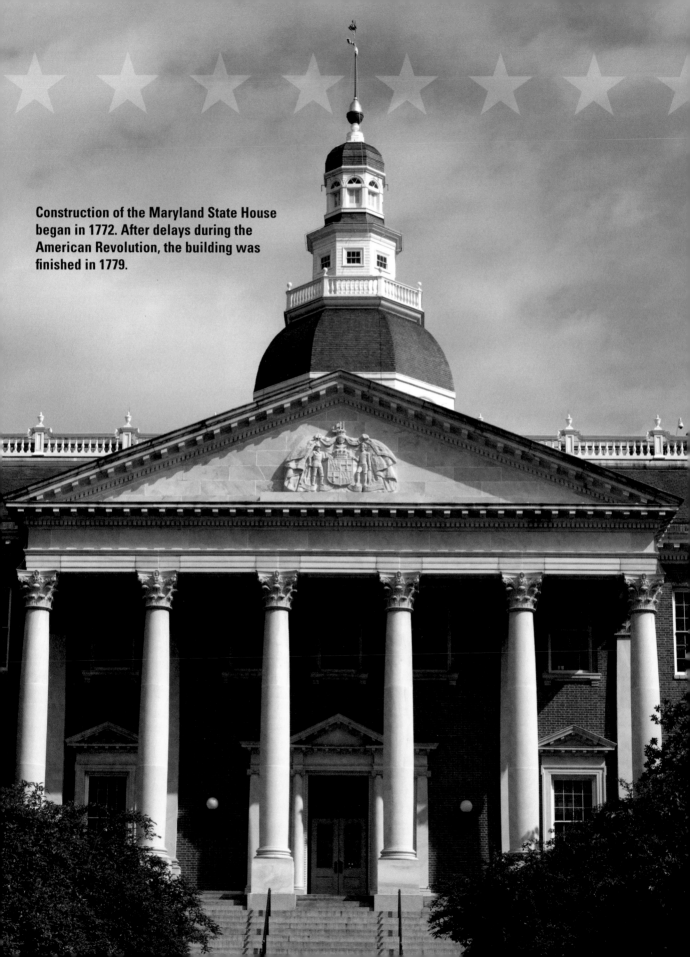

Construction of the Maryland State House began in 1772. After delays during the American Revolution, the building was finished in 1779.

How the Government Works

Like all states, Maryland has different levels of government: town or city, county, and state. At each level, the government makes and enforces laws for its residents. For Maryland counties there are three forms of government: county commisioners, code home rule, or charter.

Local Government

Maryland is divided into 23 counties. In each county, one city or town is the county seat. Elected officials meet there to make county laws. City **councils** or county commissioners enforce the laws. The county government runs some towns and cities that are unincorporated. An unincorporated community does not have its own government. It does not have its own police department and other services and must rely on the county to provide them. Towns and cities that are incorporated are run by their own governments.

Baltimore, Maryland's largest city, is not part of a county. It is an independent municipality run by a mayor and a city council. That is unusual, except in Virginia. Outside of Virginia the United States has only three independent cities: Baltimore; St. Louis, Missouri; and Carson City, Nevada.

The interior of the house of delegates chamber in the State House in Annapolis.

State Government

The state government has a similar structure to that of the federal (national) government. Both are divided into an executive branch, a legislative branch, and a judicial branch. The Maryland state constitution functions much like the U.S. Constitution. It describes the structure and rules of the state government. The state constitution that Maryland uses today has been in place since 1867.

Branches of Government

Executive

The governor is the head of the executive branch. He or she carries out laws and appoints people to high office. The governor is elected to a four-year term. He or she can serve only two terms in a row.

Legislative

This branch makes the state's laws. Maryland's legislature is called the General Assembly. It is divided into two parts. The senate has 47 members, and the house of delegates has

141 members. All General Assembly members are elected to four-year terms. There is no limit on the number of terms they can serve.

Judicial

The judicial branch **interprets** and enforces the laws. When a person is accused of breaking a law, he or she goes on trial in one of twelve district or eight circuit courts. If someone is found guilty, the case can be appealed before the court of special appeals. If he or she is found guilty again, the person can take the case to the court of appeals. This is the highest court in the state, with seven judges.

Annapolis–A Capital City

Annapolis has been Maryland's capital since 1694. "In a few years it will probably be one of the best built cities in America," one English visitor wrote in 1769. Annapolis is one of the oldest state capitals. The governor lives there, and the general assembly meets in the State House for a period of 90 days, beginning each January. Annapolis's State House is the oldest continuously used state house in the nation.

This mansion is the official home of Maryland's governor.

Annapolis was the nation's capital for a short time—from November 1783 to August 1784 —after the Treaty of Paris was signed there, which ended the Revolutionary War. Then, on December 23, 1783, George Washington resigned as commander-in-chief of the Continental Army in Annapolis. After that, the capital was moved to Trenton, New Jersey, and later to New York City and then Philadelphia. In 1789, Maryland and Virginia gave land for a permanent capital city, Washington, D.C.

In Washington, D.C.

Like all citizens, the people of Maryland are represented in the U.S. Congress in Washington, D.C. Each state elects two U.S. senators, who serve six-year terms. There is no limit on the number of terms a U.S. senator can serve.

A state's population determines the number of people that it sends to the U.S. House of Representatives. In 2014, Maryland had eight representatives in the House. They each serve two-year terms and can be elected as many times as voters choose.

How a Bill Becomes a Law

Have you ever wondered how laws are made? They often start out as the ideas of the state's residents. When people think of new laws, they can contact their representatives in the General Assembly. The representatives then write up a proposal called a bill. A bill can start in either the senate or the house of delegates. If a bill is introduced in the house of delegates, it is read before the whole house. The bill is then presented to the president of the house of delegates, who assigns the bill to a committee. It is the committee's responsibility to hold a hearing to discuss the bill. The committee may amend, or change, the bill. The committee may reject the bill and decide not to present it to the entire house. If the committee members approve the bill, it is sent back to the house. All members of the house of delegates vote on the bill.

If more than half the house members approve the bill, it goes to the state senate. There, it is discussed, debated, and voted on again. If the

In Their Own Words

"In times of adversity—for the country we love—Maryland always chooses to move forward. Progress is a choice. Job creation is a choice. Whether we move forward or back: this too is a choice."—Governor Martin O'Malley

senate approves the bill, it is then presented to the governor. He or she may sign the bill or veto, or reject, it. If the governor signs it, the bill officially becomes a state law. Even if the governor vetoes the bill, it still has a chance to become a law. The rejected bill goes back to the house and senate for a new vote. If two-thirds of both the house and senate vote to overturn the veto, the bill becomes a law.

In 2011, Governor Martin O'Malley vetoed a bill that would allow attorneys and others to copy legal forms that are generally signed and sealed, and therefore protected. In February 2014, O'Malley threatened to veto the Poultry Fair Share Act, which would force large poultry producers to help pay for cleaning up the Chesapeake Bay. He wants large companies to know that he is on their side. On the other hand, many people feel that these large companies should help clean up the pollution to which they contributed. The bill, however, was quickly withdrawn.

Governor Martin O'Malley signs a bill into law.

POLITICAL FIGURES
FROM MARYLAND

Spiro T. Agnew: Vice President of the United States, 1969-1973

Spiro Agnew was born and raised in Baltimore. After studying law, Agnew entered politics. He was elected the Governor of Maryland in 1966, and he became Vice President of the United States in 1969. In 1973, Agnew became the second Vice President to resign from office after he was charged with accepting bribes.

Thurgood Marshall: U.S. Supreme Court Justice, 1967-1991

NAACP attorney Thurgood Marshall, from Baltimore, was a leader in the fight for civil rights. In 1967, President Lyndon Johnson appointed Marshall to the U.S. Supreme Court. He was the first African American to receive that honor. Marshall served on the Court for 24 years.

Nancy Pelosi: 60th Speaker of the U.S. House of Representatives, 2007-2011

Nancy Pelosi was born in 1940 in Baltimore, Maryland. Besides raising five children, she was active in politics and won her first election to the U.S. House of Representatives in 1987. In 2007, she became the first woman to be Speaker of the House, the top job in that branch of Congress.

MARYLAND
YOU CAN MAKE A DIFFERENCE

Contacting Lawmakers

Marylanders who want to express their opinions about an issue that affects their community can visit the official state website at:

www.maryland.gov

Click on the "State Legislature" link. From there, go to the "Contact or Find a Legislator" pages. Follow the steps to find the name and contact information for any state legislator.

Chesapeake Bay Foundation

Getting Involved

Lawmakers are not the only people who have a say in Maryland's government. Ordinary citizens can do more than suggest ideas to their representatives and vote in elections. They can form citizens' groups and other organizations that promote change. Many people in Maryland are worried about the future. They see the state getting more and more crowded. New homes and business developments are taking up remaining open space. That space could be used for parks and other recreational areas.

In 1994, people who were concerned about Maryland's future got together. They did not want their state to lose all its open land to homes and businesses, so they formed a group called 1000 Friends of Maryland. The group included businesspeople and environmental groups. Like many activist groups, 1000 Friends of Maryland wants to make the state a better place. They want the government to fix up existing neighborhoods instead of tearing them down. They want to see the government carefully plan new communities without destroying the small amount of open space left in the state.

Another group, the Chesapeake Bay Foundation, fights to make the bay as clean and healthy as it was centuries ago. The group monitors the bay and shares what it learns with businesses, the public, and the government. The group also fights for tougher laws to protect and restore the bay.

Crabbing is a big part of Maryland's economy.

Making a Living

Making a living in Maryland can be hard work. But most Marylanders are not complaining. In 2012, Maryland residents earned the highest average income in the nation.

What do they do? Maryland has many doctors, mathematicians, biologists, and other scientists who do a lot of research and development. In fact, Maryland ranks second in the country in the percentage of scientists, technicians, and other professional workers. Around 8.6 percent of Maryland workers have jobs in technology. Some work at the many federal agencies headquartered in the state. They may be employed at the Agricultural Research Service in Beltsville, where they work to improve farms. Others are involved in monitoring the weather at the National Weather Service in Silver Spring. Still others work under contract for the government in one of the several research parks that dot the state. The research parks are like college campuses where many companies and institutions can share information on new technologies.

Other Marylanders work in shipping. Foreign goods come and go in the big Port of Baltimore. The port specializes in a kind of cargo transportation called roll-on/roll-off. It is the leading importer of trucks, including farm and construction equipment, which can

Baltimore is the center for business in Maryland.

be driven, or "rolled," off the ship and onto the dock. Baltimore is a good location, because it is within a day's drive of the entire Midwest and its many farms. The port is also the nation's leading importer of timber, sugar, and iron ore.

Other Marylanders work in service industries, such as hotels, restaurants, hospitals, resorts, museums, and schools. Some of them serve tourists who spend billions of dollars a year in the state. In 2012, about 27 million tourists spent $14.9 billion in the state.

Agriculture

Farming is big business in Maryland. Farms cover about a third of the state. Tobacco was once the most important crop in Maryland. In 1698, minister Hugh Jones of Calvert County wrote, "Tobacco is our meat, drink, clothing and monies." This is no longer true. As more Americans understand the harmful effects of smoking cigarettes, tobacco sales are falling. There are fewer than a hundred tobacco farms left, most of which are in the southern part of the state.

Chickens feed at a farm near Salisbury.

★10★KEY INDUSTRIES★

Agriculture

Research

Electronics

1. Aerospace and Defense

Sixteen of the top twenty-five aerospace companies and seventy of the top one hundred defense contractors in the United States are located in Maryland. Some of the top jobs in these fields include engineers, computer scientists, and technicians.

2. Agriculture

Agriculture is one of the largest commercial industries in Maryland. Around 2 million acres (809,371 ha), or roughly 32 percent, of total land area is used for farming. Chickens are one of Maryland's most important agricultural products. In 2011, the state produced nearly 311 million chicken broilers.

3. Chemical Products

Fertilizer is one of the leading chemical products made in Maryland. Other important chemical products are construction materials, soap, and paint.

4. Education and Research

Maryland has around sixty colleges and four hundred research centers. With more than $11 million in investments by the federal government, the state ranks second in the nation for annual funding for research and development.

5. Electronics

From airplane equipment and high-tech weapons to everyday cell phones, Maryland makes the electronics that change the world. Companies produce billions of dollars' worth of products each year.

MARYLAND ★ ★ ★ ★

6. Fishing

Maryland's fishing industry contributes around $600 million to the state's economy. Striped bass, white perch, and menhaden are three of the many kinds of fish caught in the Chesapeake Bay. Shark, bluefish, and flounder are harvested off the Atlantic coast.

7. Government

State government is a large employer in Maryland. With the state's proximity to the capital of the United States, Washington D.C., many residents of Maryland work for the federal government as well.

8. Healthcare

Maryland is home to around fifty short term-care hospitals and around 23,000 doctors. The healthcare industry employs nearly 276,000 people. Johns Hopkins Hospital, in Baltimore, is often ranked as one of the best hospitals in the United States.

9. Manufacturing

Around 128,000 people in Maryland are employed in manufacturing. Other than chemicals and electronics, other major products that Maryland produces are food and beverages, plastic, and rubber.

10. Tourism

Tourism is a big business in Maryland. More than 27 million people visit Maryland each year. Ocean City, in particular, is a popular tourist destination. Close to 8 million visitors enjoy the busy boardwalk and white sandy beaches yearly.

Fishing

Healthcare

Tourism

Recipe for Crab Cakes

Maryland is famous for its crabs. Most people steam the shellfish, crack them open, and enjoy the soft meat inside. You can use the crabmeat to make delicious crab cakes using this easy recipe. Have an adult help you chop the ingredients.

What You Need

3/4 pound (340 g) fresh or frozen (thawed) crab, chopped

2 cups (300 g) bread crumbs

1/4 cup (60 ml) fresh parsley, chopped

2 scallions, chopped

2 tablespoons (30 ml) lemon juice

3 eggs

Dash ground red pepper

About 2 tablespoons (30 ml) olive oil

What To Do

- Combine crab with all ingredients except the olive oil.
- Shape mixture into ten 2-inch (5 cm) cakes. Cover and refrigerate for 30 minutes.
- Heat olive oil in a large skillet over medium-high heat. Have an adult help you use the stove.
- Add crab cakes a few at a time.
- Cook until both sides are browned and crisp, about 1 to 2 minutes for each side.
- Eat alone or as a sandwich with mayonnaise mixed with lemon and Old Bay Seasoning.

Flowers and shrubs grown in nurseries are leading crops in Maryland today. Corn, soybeans, and wheat are also important. Orchards in northern Maryland produce apples, peaches, and other fruits.

Chickens are the state's main livestock product. In 2011, Maryland chickens laid around 569 million eggs. Around 310 million chickens, however, are raised for eating. These chickens are called broilers. Have you ever seen chicken that is labeled "Perdue"? Many of these chickens come from the Eastern Shore of Maryland. Perdue Farms started out as a family business and is now the third-largest chicken processor in the United States.

Shell Fishing

Maryland shell fishers, known as watermen, harvest more than 42 million pounds (19 million kilograms) of shellfish, including clams and oysters, in a year. The Chesapeake Bay is famous for its blue crabs. Crab lovers claim the meat is tastier than lobster. Marylanders think so much of their favorite shellfish that in 1989 they named it the state crustacean (shellfish). The shellfish are even featured in a favorite state slogan: "Maryland is for crabs."

Each year, Marylanders catch millions of pounds of shellfish.

The F-22A Raptor is one of the many high-tech military aircraft produced by Lockheed Martin.

Professional crabbers go out into the Chesapeake Bay in their skipjacks. They catch the blue crabs in crab pots. The crab enters a trap in the pot and cannot get out.

People who catch crabs for fun may prefer the old-fashioned long-handled dip net. They wade into the water, and when they see a crab, they dip the net to catch it.

Many crabbers also use a hand line, or bait line. This is a long string or fishing line with a weight and bait—often a chicken neck—tied to one end. They lower the line into the water until it reaches the bottom. When a crab begins to nibble on the bait, the crabber carefully pulls up the line and scoops up the crab with a net.

Made in Maryland

Manufacturing was once a core part of Maryland's economy. Today, only about one of twenty workers in Maryland has a job in manufacturing. A large number of the state's manufacturers make computers and other high-tech electronics. Interstate 270 in Montgomery County is called the state's high-technology corridor. Other manufacturers package foods, create printing products, or develop chemicals.

Your kitchen spice rack may be filled with spices made by McCormick and Company. This spice company in Sparks, Maryland, was started in 1889 by 25-year-old Willoughby McCormick in a room and cellar in Baltimore.

Defense Industry

Maryland has long played an important role in national defense. The Glenn L. Martin Company in Baltimore produced the famous B-26 bomber and other aircraft that helped the United States win World War II. After a series of mergers, the company is now part of Lockheed Martin, based in Bethesda, Maryland. Hundreds of other aerospace and defense companies have offices in Maryland.

The state's military bases are also major employers. The workforce of military and civilian personnel at Fort Meade alone is around 56,000 people. The air fleet that transports the U.S. president and other important government leaders is based at Andrews Air Force Base, Maryland, not far from Washington, D.C.

Saving the Environment

Many people in Maryland are concerned about pollution. Waste from factories and sewage systems runs into rivers and the Chesapeake Bay, killing thousands of fish. Overfishing and illegal catching of fish that are too young also hurt the fishing industry. Maryland and neighboring Virginia, Pennsylvania, and Washington, D.C., have formed the Chesapeake Bay Program. The goal of this program is to clean up local waters. Open space is gradually disappearing in Maryland. The state and federal governments are working to save the land left around Baltimore and nearby Washington, D.C. They want to preserve this land for parks and other recreational areas.

Volunteers from government agencies and environmental groups work together to restore the habitat of Barren Island in the Chesapeake Bay.

MARYLAND
STATE MAP

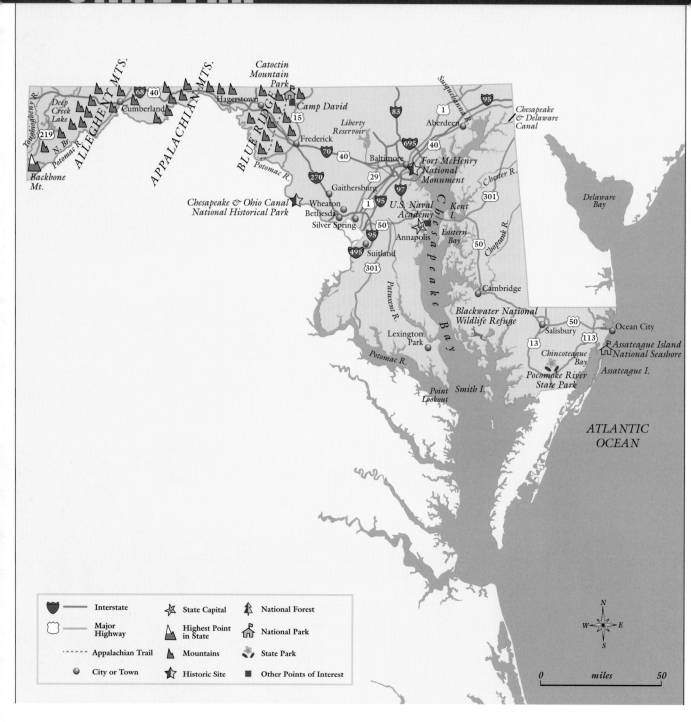

Youghiogheny R.

ALLEGHENY MTS.

Deep Creek Lake

N. Br. Potomac R.

Cumberland

219

Backbone Mt.

68 40

APPALACHIAN MTS.

Hagerstown

Catoctin Mountain Park

BLUE RIDGE

Camp David

15

Frederick

Potomac R.

70 40

270

Chesapeake & Ohio Canal National Historical Park

Wheaton

Gaithersburg

Bethesda

Silver Spring

1

29

495

301

Suitland

50

95

97

U.S. Naval Academy

Annapolis

Liberty Reservoir

83

695 40

Baltimore

Fort McHenry National Monument

Aberdeen

1

95

Susquehanna R.

Chesapeake & Delaware Canal

Chester R.

301

Kent I.

Eastern Bay

Choptank R.

50

Delaware Bay

Chesapeake Bay

Paxuxent R.

Lexington Park

Potomac R.

Point Lookout

Smith I.

Cambridge

Blackwater National Wildlife Refuge

13

Salisbury

50

113

Ocean City

Assateague Island National Seashore

Chincoteague Bay

Pocomoke River State Park

Assateague I.

ATLANTIC OCEAN

Legend

Interstate	
Major Highway	
Appalachian Trail	
City or Town	
State Capital	
Highest Point in State	
Mountains	
Historic Site	
National Forest	
National Park	
State Park	
Other Points of Interest	

N
W E
S

0   miles   50

MARYLAND ★ ★ ★

MAP SKILLS

1. What state park is located south of the city of Salisbury?

2. Which city is at the northern end of the Chesapeake Bay?

3. What is Maryland's highest point?

4. What mountain range sits between Cumberland and Hagerstown?

5. Which Interstate would you take from Frederick to Bethesda?

6. What national wildlife refuge is located south of Cambridge?

7. Ocean City is near what national park?

8. Which mountain range does the Appalachian Trail run through?

9. What point of interest is located north of Frederick?

10. Which river runs along Maryland's western border?

Fort McHenry National Monument

Cumberland

Hagerstown

10. Youghiogheny River
9. Camp David
8. Blue Ridge
7. Assateague Island National Seashore
6. Blackwater National Wildlife Refuge
5. 270
4. Appalachian
3. Backbone Mountain
2. Aberdeen
1. Pocomoke River State Park

State Seal, Flag, and Song

The front side of the state seal shows an armored Lord Baltimore on a horse. However, it is the back side of the seal that is used for official purposes. The back of the seal shows a farmer and a fisherman holding a shield with the Calvert and Crossland coats of arms.

The Maryland state flag is divided into four sections. The two black-and-gold sections represent the coat of arms of the Calvert family. The Calverts led the first English families who settled in Maryland. The red-and-white sections of the flag represent the Crossland coat of arms. Crossland was the family name of the mother of the first Lord Baltimore, George Calvert. The flag was officially adopted in 1904.

To see the lyrics of the Maryland State Song, "Maryland, My Maryland," go to **www.statesymbolsusa.org/Maryland/marylandstatesong.html**

Glossary

abolished   Officially ended or stopped.

ancestors   People who were in someone's family in past times.

councils   Groups of people who are chosen to make rules, laws, or decisions about something.

delegates   People who are chosen or elected to vote or act for others.

descendants People who come directly from earlier and usually similar individuals.

dispute   A disagreement or argument.

endangered   In danger of no longer living.

enforcement To make people obey a law.

feud   A disagreement that is usually prolonged.

interprets   Explains the meaning of.

legislature   A group of people with the power to make or change laws.

plantations   Large areas of land, especially in hot parts of the world, where crops (such as cotton) are grown.

prospered   Became strong and flourishing.

truce   An agreement between enemies or opponents to stop fighting, arguing, etc., for a certain period of time.

tuberculosis A serious disease that mainly affects the lungs.

vaccine   A substance that is usually given to a person or animal to protect against a particular disease.

More About Maryland

BOOKS

Altsheler, Joseph A. *The Sword of Antietam: A Story of the Nation's Crisis*. Whitefish, MT: Kessinger Publishing, 2010.

Blashfield, Jean F. *Maryland (America the Beautiful)*. New York, NY: Children's Press, 2014.

Cunningham, Kevin. *The Maryland Colony*. New York, NY: Scholastic, 2011.

Sanders, Nancy I. *Frederick Douglass for Kids: His Life and Times, with 21 Activities*. Chicago, IL: Chicago Review Press, 2012.

Shea, Therese. *History of the Chesapeake Bay*. New York, NY: Gareth Stevens, 2013.

WEBSITES

Maryland Kids' Page:

www.mdkidspage.org

Maryland State Archives—Guide to Government Records:

guide.mdsa.net/viewer.cfm?page=mdgov

Maryland Court System Activities and Coloring Books:

www.courts.state.md.us/publications/coloringbooks.html

ABOUT THE AUTHORS

Steven Otfinoski has written more than ninety fiction and nonfiction books for young readers. His previous works for Marshall Cavendish include books on states, history, and animals. Otfinoski lives in Connecticut with his wife, a high school teacher and an editor.

Andy Steinitz has written and edited educational and reference materials for *The World Almanac*, Borders Books, and the *New York Times*. As a child, he took trips with his family to the Eastern Shore and Baltimore's Inner Harbor. Maryland's blue crabs are one of his favorite foods. He currently works at Pratt Institute. He lives in Brooklyn, NY.

Index

Page numbers in **boldface** are illustrations.

Index